Acts of the Apostles

A Small Group Bible Study Guide

ACTS OF THE APOSTLES, A SMALL GROUP BIBLE STUDY GUIDE

© 2013 Ted LaFemina

Printed in the United States of America

ALL RIGHTS RESERVED

Scripture quotations are from:

THE HOLY BIBLE, NEW INTERNATIONAL VERSION®, NIV® Copyright © 1973, 1978, 1984, 2011 by Biblica, Inc.™ Used by permission. All rights reserved worldwide.

Scripture taken from the New King James Version®. Copyright © 1982 by Thomas Nelson, Inc. Used by permission. All rights reserved.

Published by Pressed Thoughts LLC

www.pressedthoughts.com

ISBN 978-0-9850102-2-5

CONTENTS

DEDICATION

This book is dedicated to the good men at MCI-H as well as incarcerated Christians everywhere who choose to follow Paul's example of using every opportunity within prison walls to share the love of Christ with those around them, and especially Lewis who allowed me to join him in his small group times where I witnessed the Holy Spirit in action.

Special thanks goes to Marla for her invaluable help and support in editing this guide.

THE SMALL GROUP BIBLE STUDY

The purpose of this guide is to support a short, small group Bible study of the Book of Acts. It is designed to encourage the participants to think deeper about what they are reading and also to see, through firsthand study, how the Bible, in its entirety, weaves together a tale of God's love for us.

An effective small group Bible study, however, has multiple purposes. One, of course, is to facilitate the mutual, intellectual understanding of the text under study. Another, more important aspect of the group is to build closer relationships with one another. It makes no sense to mechanically lead a small group through a study of Acts with the same determination used by General Sherman as he marched through the South. Sometimes it is important to take a break on this study of Christian love, so that you can actually engage in Christian love. So as you move through the study, do not be afraid of tangential conversations and do not be afraid to even skip the scheduled study of the day if the Spirit is leading the group to spend a little time building intimacy or helping someone work through a life issue.

The chapters of this guide break the study of Acts into six lessons; however, the questions within these chapters follow the book chronologically to enable the group to set their own pace of study. As a group, it makes sense to adjust the pace of the lessons as you go based on the level of discussion activity within each session.

As you sit down to read the scriptures prior to each of these sessions, take the time to pray that the Holy Spirit guide you in your understanding of the text. And as you meet together as a group, pray that the Holy Spirit guide the discussion in a manner pleasing to the Lord.

HOW TO STUDY A BOOK OF THE BIBLE

A book of the Bible can be studied in many different ways and a student is free to go to whatever depth of study they desire. On the shelves of bookstores, you can find that authors have written whole volumes focusing on just a single verse of the scriptures.

The style of study this guide supports is a more cursory study that should leave the student with a fair understanding of the main messages of the book, thus leaving time for the student to continue with other areas of the Bible. Many have found that after they have read through and studied larger portions of the Bible at a higher level, their ability to understand each individual book is deepened.

To facilitate this study, begin by reading the entire book, cover to cover; then, as you proceed with the lessons, read through each set of chapters again with more care. It is often helpful to make notes on what you perceive as the key points of the text. You can then read the questions within this guide, making notes and writing down answers as you go.

It is strongly recommended that a Study Bible be used for this study and in an edition that is readable for you. If you are very comfortable reading old English, or just like a challenge, then the King James version may be for you. The majority of scripture passages used in this book are from the NIV Bible, which provides

3

a very readable translation and is also an accurate translation, thought-for-thought, of the original Biblical texts.

Note that Study Bibles are meant to be *dirty* Bibles. As you read along, don't hesitate to underline meaningful verses, scribble notes in the margin, and otherwise markup your Bible.

Other Bible resources are available to aid in the study and should be used freely to help you gain further insight. Digital versions of the Bible are available online and also available for hand-held devices. These versions provide full-text word search capability that is ideal for locating and reading other passages of scripture that relate to the current study.

INTRODUCTION TO ACTS

The Acts of the Apostles was written by the physician Luke, who also wrote the Gospel of Luke. He wrote the two books to his friend Theophilus which, in Greek, means *friend of God*. It is unclear whether Theophilus. was an actual person's name, an encoded name used to protect the intended recipient from harm, or a general term for all believers. The book was likely written in 61 AD.

Acts provides the best historical account of the activities of the apostles during the early, chaotic first years of the Christian Church; however, its focus is primarily on the apostles Peter and Paul, both of whom Luke spent significant amounts of time with. From his two accounts, it is evident that Luke took time to research historical events through personal interviews with the people who knew Jesus best. Of course, it is also evident from his accounts that he spent significant time with these individuals and supported their missionary efforts, so finding time and access to them was not a challenge.

In a larger sense, the book of Acts chronicles the works of the Holy Spirit working through these two willing apostles, fulfilling, in the process, many prophecies recorded in the early scriptures as well as a few prophecies shared with the early disciples by Jesus himself.

To understand the situation, events, and thinking of the various people encountered in Luke's account, it us useful to review the history of Israel in the years leading up to Jesus.

The first few chapters of this study guide offer a brief overview of the political background of the times, the various religious groups in power, a few important messianic prophecies the Jews would have been familiar with, some prophecies Jesus made about the future during the course of his three and a half year ministry, some background information on the individual apostles, and a list of some of the important covenants God had made with his people.

POLITICAL BACKGROUND

In 586 BC, the Lord gave a disobedient Israel into the hands of King Nebuchadnezzar II of Bablyon. Most of the Jewish population, including the prophet Daniel, was relocated to Babylon. In 538 BC (Ezra 1), a new leader, Cyrus, of Babylon granted religious freedom to his captive peoples and ~50,000 Judeans, led by Zerubbabel returned to Judah to rebuild the temple. In 456 BC (Nehemiah 2), King Artaxerxes allowed Nehemiah and Ezra to return to Jerusalem to rebuild the city's wall and re-establish the city. Nehemiah and Ezra called the people to repentance and re-established the Jewish nation.

In 333 BC, Alexander the Great conquered the Persian Empire. Alexander encouraged Jews to settle in Alexandria and, about this time, the Pentateuch (the first five books of the Bible written by Moses) was translated to Greek (becoming known as the Septuagint). Alexander died in 323 BC, and several hundred years of turmoil ensued. Judea sat between the Seleucid Empire and Egypt and changed hands several times in this period. Prior to Alexander, the political and religious leadership of Judea was one and the same; however, once conquered, the nation begin to split into different philosophical groups; factionalizing the people. Some felt it was best just to follow the conquering political leaders and keep their heads; others felt it important to hold to the religion and fight for their rights, while many others sought a middle ground.

In 64 BC, the Roman general Pompey conquered the region and, in 37 BC, the Romans installed a Jewish King, Herod the Great. The Romans recognized the fanatical tendencies of the Jews and, to keep peace, allowed them to continue to practice their own religion, rather than worship Caesar as a God. The Jews were the only people in the Roman Empire who were granted this right. While Herod was Jewish (half-Jewish anyway), he was a tyrannical ruler: He used slave labor to make a name for himself by greatly expanding the temple, and he ordered his own wife and several family members executed. King Herod also ordered all the baby boys under age two killed (Matthew 2:16–18) when he heard that the Messiah had been born – he didn't want any competition. King Herod understood that his power depended on Rome's favor, so he made sure to keep Rome happy.

The average Jew, of course, was not happy. The Romans taxed heavily, and they did not truly have religious freedom. Living as a Jew in Judea at that time was probably similar in feel to living as a Christian in China today. Chinese Christians are free to worship, but only with priests approved by the state and only in churches approved by the state. They know that, at any time, the government might crack down and throw them in jail.

An important point to note is that Alexander effectively established a common language across the Mediterranean empire, and the Romans created a relatively safe and efficient transportation system and, therefore, an economic system, across the entire region. At the time of Christ, the most widely spoken language in the world was broken-Greek. Jewish communities existed in towns and cities across the entire Roman Empire, and these Jews carried with them the blended cultures and languages of their respective regions.

In the book of Leviticus (part of the Pentateuch), the Lord commands a number of feasts to be celebrated at the tabernacle (located in the temple in Jesus' day). On the Sunday of Passover week, the *Feast of the First Fruits* was to be celebrated. Then, 50 days after that, the *Feast of Pentecost* was to be celebrated. During this time, Jews from all over the world would come to Jerusalem (remember this when reading Acts 2). After Acts 2, most of the believers continued to hang out in Jerusalem, which did not really help God's overall plan of spreading the Gospel throughout the world. Bring in Paul's persecution. Paul's persecution of these first Christians caused the believing Jews to leave Jerusalem and go back to their own cities and towns, bringing the good news of Jesus (or at least their best understanding of it) with them. (Note the term *Christian* was first used a little later in history, as documented in Acts 11:26.)

Prior to this time, religious and philosophical ideas were relatively constrained by basic geography. Had the Messiah come 500 years earlier, news of it would have pretty much stayed within the tribes of Israel. It makes you begin to wonder if God had a plan.

RELIGIOUS GROUPS

As mentioned above, the years of disjoined rule within Judea caused numerous factions to develop within society. The most notable groups are discussed below.

Pharisees - Held the view that, if they followed the Law of Moses completely, they could be free of sin. They studied the scriptures carefully and codified the Mosaic Laws into 613 commandments to help them know what was, and was not, a sin. For example, Exodus 20:10 says that you should not work on the Sabbath. The Pharisees decided that healing was work, so they criticized Jesus for healing on the Sabbath (Matthew 12:10). Josephus said *the Pharisees are those who are esteemed most skillful in the exact explication of their laws.... These ascribe all to fate [or providence], and to God, and yet allow, that to act what is right, or the contrary, is principally in the power of men, although fate does cooperate in every action. They say that all souls are incorruptible, but that the souls of good men only are removed into other bodies, – but that the souls of bad men are subject to eternal punishment... Moreover, the Pharisees are friendly to one another, and are for the exercise of concord, and regard for the public.*

The Pharisees generally controlled the synagogues. Jesus criticized the Pharisees as hypocrites (Mathew 15:7).

Scribes - These were the copyists of the law, and they trained

11

rigorously. Because of this training, they were experts on the law and served as judges in legal cases. Generally, they were close to the Pharisees.

Sadducees - These were generally Jews of wealth and position. They controlled the temple and the priesthood. The Sadducees believed in the Pentateuch (the five books written by Moses) but rejected the spiritual authority of later scripture writers. Josephus described their philosophy as *those that...take away fate entirely, and suppose that God is not concerned in our doing or not doing what is evil; and they say, that to act what is good, or what is evil, is at men's own choice, and that the one or the other belongs so to every one, that they may act as they please.... the behavior of the Sadducees one towards another is in some degree wild, and their conversation with those that are of their own party is as barbarous as if they were strangers to them.*

Jesus scolded the Sadducees about failing to believe in the resurrection of the dead (Mathew 22:23-33).

Essenes - According to Josephus, *the Essens are much more severe in their beliefs than the Pharisees. According to him: [They] are Jews by birth, and seem to have a greater affection for one another than the other sects have. These Essens reject pleasures as an evil, but esteem continence, and the conquest over our passions, to be virtue.... These men are despisers of riches, and so very communicative as raises our admiration. Nor is there any one to be found among them who hath more than another; for it is a law among them, that those who come to them must let what they have be common to the whole order, - insomuch that among them all there is no appearance of poverty, or excess of riches, but every one's possessions are intermingled with every other's possessions; and so there is, as it were, one patrimony among all the brethren.*

In a way, Josephus's description of the Essenes's lifestyle seems similar to that described by the early Christians in the opening of Acts; however, Josephus also documents a form of discipline they use which seems severe: *But for those that are caught in any heinous sins, they cast them out of their society; and he who is thus separated from them does often die after a miserable manner; for as he is bound by the oath he hath taken, and by the customs he hath been engaged in, he is not at liberty to partake of that food that he meets with elsewhere, but is forced to eat grass, and to famish his body with hunger, till he perish; for which reason they receive many of them again when they are at their last gasp, out of compassion to them, as thinking the miseries they have endured till they came to the very brink of death to be a sufficient punishment for the sins they had been guilty of.*

Herodians - This group believed it simplest and best to cooperate with Rome.

It's interesting to compare the American occupation of Afghanistan to the Roman occupation of Judea at the time of Christ. America, like Rome, was attempting to create a stable, peaceable region that could participate in a global economic system. The Taliban, following the hard-core Wahhabi view of Islam, are like the Pharisees, trying to please God by strictly following all the rules. Moderate Islamists, like the Sadducees, want power but want to keep their TV's and clothes as well. The rest of Afghanistan, like the Herodians, figure that American democracy isn't so bad as long as they can live in peace.

Note that each of these different groups had a set of beliefs that corresponded with their worldview. But is it our beliefs that define our worldview, or our worldview that define our beliefs? It seems that the answer is frequently neither. All of us have an inner desire to feel significant, important, and valued; we have a tendency to define for ourselves a worldview that allows us to most easily satisfy this desire, and we accept only those beliefs that fit into our constructed worldview. As we get older, we tend to lose the motivational energy to grow and change and, therefore, we find it hard to accept any new beliefs or ideas that would force us to re-think our own personal, logical structure of the world. Physiologists have shown that humans have a very strong natural tendency to hold fast to any decisions that they have previously made.

Jesus didn't fit into the worldview of any of the groups. Jesus demanded that people grow, learn, and change! Jesus also didn't accept that anyone was "good enough" on their own: He saw the hypocrisy of the Pharisees, he saw the love of power in the Sadducees, and he rejected them all. Jesus demanded that people be willing to give up everything that they used to define their own personal success and importance and, instead, look to him for true value. However, the Pharisees of the day would not give up their place of honor in society, and the Sadducees would not give up their power so, together, they had the redeemer of the world crucified.

Are the demands of Jesus any different for us today, than they were for the people in that day?

What is it that makes you feel important, valued, and successful? (Hint: What is it that you spend your time and money on?) Are any of these things keeping you from opening your heart and accepting all that Christ has to offer you?

Do you find yourself continually open to new understanding from the scriptures as revealed to you by the Holy Spirit, or do you find that you simply look for those passages that already fit into your worldview? Do you humble yourself and ask the Holy Spirit to guide you or do you think you have God all figured out already?

A DAY IN THE LIFE OF THE ROMAN AUTHORITIES

Aside from Acts, the best source of information about the life in times in Judea during this critical juncture in its history was Josephus, a Jewish historian, who wrote several books documenting the last days of the Jewish age.

It is hard to imagine how difficult it must have been to be the designated Roman ruler of the region. Rome appointed Jews as kings in the region in an attempt to keep some semblance of peace. The Jews they picked were puppet kings who gained their power through political maneuvering within the Roman system. In Luke's account of Acts, we meet three of these rulers, Felix, Festus, and Agrippa II. The following anecdote, recorded by Josephus, gives just a glimpse of the types of issues these rulers had to deal with on a day-to-day basis in Judea.

Now after the death of Herod, king of Chalcis, Claudius set Agrippa, the son of Agrippa, over his uncle's kingdom, while Cumanus took upon him the office of procurator of the rest, which was a Roman province, and therein he succeeded Alexander; under which Cureanus began the troubles, and the Jews' ruin came on; for when the multitude were come together to Jerusalem, to the feast of unleavened bread, and a Roman cohort stood over the cloisters of the temple, (for they always were armed, and kept guard at the festivals, to prevent any innovation which the multitude thus gathered together might make,) one of the soldiers pulled back his garment, and cowering down after an indecent manner, turned his breech to the Jews, and spake such words as you might expect upon such a posture. At this the whole multitude had indignation, and made a clamor to Cumanus, that he would punish the soldier; while the rasher part of the youth, and such as were naturally the most tumultuous, fell to fighting, and caught up stones, and threw them at the soldiers. Upon which Cumanus was afraid lest all the people should make an assault upon him, and sent to call for more armed men, who, when they came in great numbers into the cloisters, the Jews were in a very great consternation; and being beaten out of the temple, they ran into the city; and the violence with which they crowded to get out was so great, that they trod upon each other, and squeezed one another, till ten thousand of them were killed, insomuch that this feast became the cause of mourning to the whole nation, and every family lamented their own relations.

MESSIANIC PROPHECIES

The prophecies recorded in the ancient scriptures were often spiritual visions that the various human prophets attempted to record, using the language of their times. To understand how difficult this is, try to explain colorful artwork to someone who has been color-blind from birth. At the time of Christ, as now, there were various disagreements as to the meaning of prophecies, or even which scriptures were prophetic. Nevertheless, the fanatical devotion to the study of the scriptures (both then and now) cannot be underestimated and there was, and is, general consensus on many of the prophecies.

An important Messianic prophet was Daniel. In Chapter 9 of his book, he predicted that, from the time that the word went out to restore and rebuild Jerusalem (~456 BC) until the time of an anointed prince, would be 49 years (or ~407 BC). And in 434 years (or ~27AD) *it shall be built again with streets and moat, but in a troubled time.*

The Jewish people in the days of Jesus were aware of this prophecy. Some interpreted it to refer to previous events, but many expected a Messiah to show up sometime soon. Many looked forward to the Messiah to deliver them from Rome; they looked at prophecies like those quoted below from Micah and Psalms, expecting that the Messiah would come as a mighty warrior and help them "break the Romans to pieces":

17

"In that day," declares the LORD, "I will gather the lame; I will assemble the exiles and those I have brought to grief. I will make the lame a remnant, those driven away a strong nation. **The LORD will rule over them in Mount Zion from that day and forever.** *As for you, O watchtower of the flock,* **O stronghold of the Daughter of Zion, the former dominion will be restored to you; kingship will come to the Daughter of Jerusalem."** *Why do you now cry aloud-- have you no king? Has your counselor perished, that pain seizes you like that of a woman in labor? Writhe in agony, O Daughter of Zion, like a woman in labor, for now you must leave the city to camp in the open field. You will go to Babylon; there you will be rescued.* **There the LORD will redeem you out of the hand of your enemies.** *But now many nations are gathered against you. They say, "Let her be defiled, let our eyes gloat over Zion!" But they do not know the thoughts of the LORD; they do not understand his plan, he who gathers them like sheaves to the threshing floor.* **"Rise and thresh, O Daughter of Zion, for I will give you horns of iron; I will give you hoofs of bronze and you will break to pieces many nations."** *You will devote their ill-gotten gains to the LORD, their wealth to the Lord of all the earth.*

– Micah 4 (~700 BC)

Endow the king with your justice, O God, the royal son with your righteousness. He will judge your people in righteousness, your afflicted ones with justice. The mountains will bring prosperity to the people, the hills the fruit of righteousness. **He will defend the afflicted among the people and save the children of the needy; he will crush the oppressor.** *He will endure as long as the sun, as long as the moon, through all generations. He will be like rain falling on a mown field, like showers watering the earth.* **In his days the righteous will flourish; prosperity will abound till the moon is no more. He will rule from sea to sea and from the River to the ends of the earth. The desert tribes will bow before him and his enemies will lick the dust.** *The kings of Tarshish and of distant shores will bring tribute to him; the kings of Sheba and Seba will present him gifts.* **All kings will bow down to him and all nations will serve him.**

– Psalm 72 (~950 BC)

There were, however, a number of other prophecies, which

must have been harder to understand. These prophecies showed a humbler Messiah. For example:

Rejoice greatly, O Daughter of Zion! Shout, Daughter of Jerusalem! **See, your king comes to you, righteous and having salvation, gentle and riding on a donkey,** *on a colt, the foal of a donkey.*
– Zechariah 9 (~520 BC)

The Messiah comes gentle and riding on a donkey? What kind of warrior king is this?

Nevertheless, there will be no more gloom for those who were in distress. In the past he humbled the land of Zebulun and the land of Naphtali, **but in the future he will honor Galilee of the Gentiles, by the way of the sea, along the Jordan** *– The people walking in darkness have seen a great light; on those living in the land of the shadow of death a light has dawned. You have enlarged the nation and increased their joy; they rejoice before you as people rejoice at the harvest, as men rejoice when dividing the plunder. For as in the day of Midian's defeat, you have shattered the yoke that burdens them, the bar across their shoulders, the rod of their oppressor. Every warrior's boot used in battle and every garment rolled in blood will be destined for burning, will be fuel for the fire.* **For to us a child is born, to us a son is given, and the government will be on his shoulders.** *And he will be called Wonderful Counselor, Mighty God, Everlasting Father, Prince of Peace. Of the increase of his government and peace there will be no end. He will reign on David's throne and over his kingdom, establishing and upholding it with justice and righteousness from that time on and forever. The zeal of the LORD Almighty will accomplish this.*
– Isaiah 9:1-9 (~690 BC)

The last bit sounds good, but the bit about honoring Galilee of the Gentiles? That doesn't make sense. Shouldn't it be the Jews in Jerusalem? And the part about a child being born? Who talks about the warrior king as a child?

[God] says: "It is too small a thing for you to be my servant to restore the tribes of Jacob and bring back those of Israel I have kept. **I will also make you a light for the Gentiles, that you may bring my salvation to the ends of the earth."**

– Isaiah 49:6 (~690 BC)

If the Jews, the children of Abraham, are God's chosen people, what is this talk about the Messiah being "a light to the Gentiles"? Isn't he supposed to be *our* God?

But he was pierced for our transgressions, he was crushed for our iniquities; the punishment that brought us peace was upon him, and by his wounds we are healed. *We all, like sheep, have gone astray, each of us has turned to his own way; and the LORD has laid on him the iniquity of us all.* **He was oppressed and afflicted,** *yet he did not open his mouth;* **he was led like a lamb to the slaughter,** *and as a sheep before her shearers is silent, so he did not open his mouth. By oppression and judgment he was taken away. And who can speak of his descendants? For he was cut off from the land of the living; for the transgression of my people he was stricken.* **He was assigned a grave with the wicked,** *and with the rich in his death, though he had done no violence, nor was any deceit in his mouth. Yet* **it was the LORD's will to crush him and cause him to suffer,** *and though the LORD makes his life a guilt offering, he will see his offspring and prolong his days, and the will of the LORD will prosper in his hand. After the suffering of his soul, he will see the light [of life] and be satisfied; by his knowledge my righteous servant will justify many, and he will bear their iniquities. Therefore I will give him a portion among the great, and he will divide the spoils with the strong, because he poured out his life unto death, and was numbered with the transgressors. For he bore the sin of many, and made intercession for the transgressors.*
– Isaiah 53:5-12 (~690 BC)

The Messiah gets pierced and suffers? He gets put into a grave with the wicked? What's up with this?

"The time is coming," *declares the* LORD, **"when I will make a new covenant with the house of Israel and with the house of Judah.** *It will not be like the covenant I made with their forefathers when I took them by the hand to lead them out of Egypt, because they broke my covenant, though I was a husband to them,* "declares the LORD. *"This is the covenant I will make with the house of Israel after that time,"* *declares the* LORD. **"I will put my law in their minds and write it on their hearts. I will be their God, and they will be my people. No longer will a man teach his neighbor,** *or a man his brother, saying,*

'Know the LORD,' because they will all know me, from the least of them to the greatest," declares the LORD. "For I will forgive their wickedness and will remember their sins no more."

– Jeremiah 31 (~600 BC)

A new covenant where God's law is written in our minds and hearts? No need for the Pharisees to go around teaching us the rules? The old covenant becomes obsolete? Does this make any sense?

These scriptures were well known to the Jews of the time, even to the Jews of Galilee. The teaching tradition of the Jews was a questioning one (Luke 2:46-47). That is, the elders or teachers of the law would badger students with questions, forcing them to remember and to think through their answers. Traditionally, the students were first taught the book of Leviticus and then the rest of the Pentateuch; the focus of teaching was not on academics and culture, but rather to know and fear the Lord. It's easy to see, though, where many would focus on those scriptures offering hope of victory over Rome and treat lightly these other, harder-to-understand verses.

Above, we talked about the prophecy of Daniel in Chapter 9. The next few sentences are interesting:

After the [434 years] (e.g. 27 AD), an anointed one shall be cut off and shall have nothing, and the troops of the prince who is to come shall destroy the city and the sanctuary. Its end shall come with a flood, and to the end there shall be war. Desolations are decreed. He shall make a strong covenant with many for [seven years], and for half of the [period] (e.g. 3½ years) he shall make sacrifice and offering cease; and in their place shall be an abomination that desolates, until the decreed end is poured out upon the desolator.

Note that Jesus' ministry started around 27 AD, and he was crucified (pierced) after sharing the good news for 3½ years, in 31 AD. At the last supper, Jesus did make a new, everlasting covenant with all believers, and his personal sacrifice and offering was the final one, atoning for our transgressions forever.

JESUS' PROPHECIES

Jesus, of course, was a prophet himself, and he shared a number of prophecies with his disciples that they found difficult to imagine or understand at the time.

Then the Jews demanded of him, "What miraculous sign can you show us to prove your authority to do all this?" Jesus answered them, "Destroy this temple, and I will raise it again in three days." The Jews replied, "It has taken forty-six years to build this temple, and you are going to raise it in three days?"
– John 18-20

This one took on new meaning for the apostles after he rose from the dead in three days. When do you think they first remembered him saying it?

"I have much more to say to you, more than you can now bear. But when he, the Spirit of truth, comes, he will guide you into all truth. He will not speak on his own; he will speak only what he hears, and he will tell you what is yet to come. He will bring glory to me by taking from what is mine and making it known to you. All that belongs to the Father is mine. That is why I said the Spirit will take from what is mine and make it known to you. "In a little while you will see me no more, and then after a little while you will see me."
– John 16:12-16

Jesus had much more to say, but he'll let the Spirit say it? What exactly did he mean by that? What does he have to say? What does it mean, "all that belongs to the Father will be made know to us"?

Jesus left the temple and was walking away when his disciples came up to him to call his attention to its buildings. **"Do you see all these things?" he asked. "I tell you the truth, not one stone here will be left on another; every one will be thrown down."** *As Jesus was sitting on the Mount of Olives, the disciples came to him privately. "Tell us," they said, "when will this happen, and what will be the sign of your coming and of the end of the age?" Jesus answered: "Watch out that no one deceives you. For many will come in my name, claiming, 'I am the Christ, ' and will deceive many. You will hear of wars and rumors of wars, but see to it that you are not alarmed. Such things must happen, but the end is still to come. Nation will rise against nation, and kingdom against kingdom. There will be famines and earthquakes in various places. All these are the beginning of birth pains.* **"Then you will be handed over to be persecuted and put to death, and you will be hated by all nations because of me.** *At that time many will turn away from the faith and will betray and hate each other, and many false prophets will appear and deceive many people. Because of the increase of wickedness, the love of most will grow cold, but* **he who stands firm to the end will be saved. And this gospel of the kingdom will be preached in the whole world as a testimony to all nations, and then the end will come.** *"So when you see standing in the holy place 'the abomination that causes desolation,' spoken of through the prophet Daniel--let the reader understand-- then let those who are in Judea flee to the mountains. Let no one on the roof of his house go down to take anything out of the house. Let no one in the field go back to get his cloak. How dreadful it will be in those days for pregnant women and nursing mothers! Pray that your flight will not take place in winter or on the Sabbath. For then there will be great distress, unequaled from the beginning of the world until now--and never to be equaled again. If those days had not been cut short, no one would survive, but for the sake of the elect those days will be shortened. At that time if anyone says to you, 'Look, here is the Christ!' or, 'There he is!' do not believe it. For false Christs and false prophets will appear and perform great signs and miracles to deceive even the elect--if that were possible. See, I have told you ahead of time. "So if anyone tells you, 'There he is, out in the desert,' do not go out; or, 'Here he is, in the inner rooms,' do not believe it.* **For as lightning that comes from the east is visible even in the west, so will be the coming of the Son of Man.** *Wherever there is a carcass, there the vultures will gather. "Immediately after the distress of those*

24

days " 'the sun will be darkened, and the moon will not give its light; the stars will fall from the sky, and the heavenly bodies will be shaken.' "At that time the sign of the Son of Man will appear in the sky, and all the nations of the earth will mourn. They will see the Son of Man coming on the clouds of the sky, with power and great glory. And he will send his angels with a loud trumpet call, and they will gather his elect from the four winds, from one end of the heavens to the other. "Now learn this lesson from the fig tree: As soon as its twigs get tender and its leaves come out, you know that summer is near. Even so, when you see all these things, you know that it is near, right at the door. **I tell you the truth, this generation will certainly not pass away until all these things have happened.** *Heaven and earth will pass away, but my words will never pass away.*

– Mathew 24

During the time of Acts, these words caused many to expect the second coming of Christ very soon, and they made decisions to that effect, but did they really understand the passage? Note that the historical records of the events leading up to the destruction of the temple in 70 AD provide reasonably convincing evidence that this prophecy was fulfilled at that time; of course, scholarly debate continues over the interpretations of Mathew 24.

In Acts 1, we learn that Jesus asked the disciples to "wait in Jerusalem" to be baptized by the Holy Spirit. In this time of waiting, what must have been going through their minds? Would they be remembering these prophecies? How much could they have really understood at that time? How much do we really understand even now? How much do we actually have to understand in order to please God?

THE APOSTLES

A theme throughout the Bible is that we should look to the Lord for glory, power, and righteousness, rather than ourselves. Whenever God has something to accomplish, he always seems to want to do it through very humble folks so that it is clear to everyone that God is the one in control (Judges 7:2-3). The apostles, with the unique exception of Paul, fit into this category. Most were basically uneducated peasants; the one thing that sets them apart is that they had true hearts for the Lord, and they seemed to recognize and want to follow the Lord shortly after meeting him. Contrast these men with the Pharisees who actually witnessed Jesus heal a shriveled hand right in front of them and still wanted to arrest him.

While the apostles had good hearts, they also had very uneducated hearts. We struggle to understand the true meaning of the Gospels today, and many of us have advanced educations; we have the benefit of printed copies of the Bible (with handy cross-reference systems and a concordance in the back). We have the *New Testament* (canon defined in 367 AD), we've listened to sermons, and we can do full-text Bible searches from our wireless 4G phones. Most importantly, we have 2000 years of academic and philosophic teaching to lean on. We have phrases like "the Holy Trinity" – coined in the 3rd century, and "substitutionary atonement" – coined in the 12th century. At the time of Christ's crucifixion, the apostles had none of this. All they had was their time spent with Christ, during which John and James wanted to call down thunder and lightning from heaven to destroy a city (after which Jesus nicknamed them "Sons of Thunder") Peter tried to defend Jesus by hacking the ear off a soldier (the Lord almighty couldn't defend himself?), and of course Peter had also denied knowing Christ just a few hours after swearing that he would never do so. Even at the last supper, the apostles were arguing with themselves as to which one of them would be most important in heaven.

How could this unlikely group of men change the world?

To get a little better insight into the individual apostles that sat huddled together, waiting patiently for whatever the Lord was going to send them, a brief bio on each of these apostles is included below.

Peter (Simon) – A simple fisherman (owned his own fishing business). He lived in a simple home, in Bethsaida in Galilee, with his mother-in-law. His wife probably died early. The stories in John 21:5-8 and 14:25-31 give the impression that Peter was a bit like Forest Gump sometimes – always leading with his heart, rather than his head. However, you can see, in the accounts of Luke, that he frequently displayed the kind of initiative and leadership found in small-business owners today.

Andrew – Peter's brother, also a simple fisherman, lived with his brother. The few references to Andrew's behavior, as recorded in the gospels, show him introducing individuals, one at a time, to Jesus.

Mathew (Levi) – A roman tax collector. Rome sold the rights to collect tax to the highest bidder. The Tax collectors then overtaxed the population to make their money – and the Jews hated them for it. Tax collectors were educated, financially savvy, and shrewd. Mathew owned a large villa in Capharnaum and also a "tax collector's palace" just outside a city. Tax collectors could rise to higher social and political status than other Jewish people of the time could.

Thomas – A simple fisherman, likely did not own his own business, but was a poor laborer for another. The gospels portray him as full of love, melancholy, and courage. Heading into Jerusalem, he had realistic fears of what might happen. He was the last apostle to see the risen Christ, but the first to recognize him as God.

Philip – Also lived in the small fishing town of Bethsaida, but his career isn't mentioned. He was quick on money calculations – with one glance, it was clear to him that *two hundred denarii worth of bread is not enough for them, that each one many receive a little.* (John 6:6-7 NKJV). Philip didn't grasp the philosophical, big-picture ideas so much; he appeared to be a bit more anal-retentive.

Bartholomew (Nathanael) – A friend of Philip. A devout Jew from Cana in Galilee. Bartholomew was probably also a fisherman.

John – A fisherman from Bethsaida who worked for his father, Zebedee. The gospel evidence indicates that Zebedee had some measure of wealth and status (John had access to the high priest's house). John & James's mother, Salome, was a believer and witness to the crucifixion, ministered to Jesus during his ministry, and brought spices to anoint Jesus' body after his burial. John took care of Jesus' mother Mary after the crucifixion. From Luke 9:52-56, you can get the impression that John and his brother James were a bit like a bulls in a china shop. In later years, after the crucifixion, John mellowed significantly.

James – Brother of John, he also worked for his father.

Simon "the Cananean" or "the Zealot" – Note that *Cananean* is Aramaic for *zealot*. Not much is written about Simon, however, the historian Josephus describes the Zealots as a political group that believed Israel should be ruled by God alone and, therefore, worked to fight Rome through various guerila style attacks. It is interesting to consider that both Simon, the Zealot, and Mathew, who collected taxes for Rome, were both selected by Jesus.

Jude (Thaddeus) – Little is know of Jude. Scholars speculate that he was a farmer by trade because that was the prevailing occupation in the region. There is disagreement as to whether the apostle Jude is the same person as Jude, the brother of Jesus (see Mark 6:3). Many scholars do not believe the apostle Jude was the same person as the Jude that penned the New Testament Epistle of Jude.

James "the less" or "the younger" – James' mother was also a witness to the crucifixion and, along with Mary Magdalene, was a witness of Jesus' burial. The gospel's indicate that both James and Mathew had a father named Alphaeus and so the two may have been brothers.

Paul (Saul) – A Pharisee from the tribe of Benjamin who studied under Gamaliel, a preeminent teacher of the day. Saul was a Roman citizen by birth; his rights as a Roman citizen protected him on more than one occasion. Paul was multilingual and versed in the customs of both the Jews and Gentiles, allowing him to be quite effective in his preaching wherever he traveled.

As for why God chose Paul? Look at his heart and his motivations. It is interesting to compare Paul to David. King David, if you read the accounts written of him (1 Samuel 27, 2 Samuel 16:5-13, 1 Kings 2:8-9), could be classified as a terrorist. However, David loved the Lord and always looked to him for guidance – he never turned anywhere else. As I look back and read of his actions, David seems to have had terribly poor judgment but, in David's eyes, he felt he was doing right by the Lord and the Lord loved him for it. Paul is pretty much the same way and, unlike the other Pharisees, when Paul was actually confronted with the Lord, he recognized and submitted to the Lord immediately. For this, Jesus loved him.

THE COVENANTS OF GOD

God made several contracts (covenants) with the Israelites over the course of their history, and they felt pride in being God's special people.   Of course, the Bible narrative tells us that the Israelites regularly failed to keep their side of these contracts and were severely punished because of it (the exile to Babylon being the prime example).   God frequently felt like a husband whose wife cheats on him (Jeremiah 3:6-10).   Because of these punishments, the more devout Jews felt it very important to remember and keep their side of the contracts.   Paul may have been the first scholar to understand that Jesus established a new covenant, which makes these old covenants obsolete; however, it's hard to change a theological worldview that is ingrained in every fiber of your being. It is worth reviewing these covenants to help build an understanding of the mindset of the Jews of the day.

With Noah (Gen 9) – God promised that He would no longer destroy the whole world by flood. The rainbow is a sign of this covenant.

With Abraham (Gen 17) – God promised to bless Abraham's descendants, making him father to many nations; his descendants as numerous as the stars. God promised to be their God and they would be His People (Lev 26). In return, Abraham's male descendants must all be circumcised as a reminder of the covenant.

With Moses (Ex 19) – God offered to make the Israelites his treasured possession, to make them a kingdom of priests, and a holy nation. In return, they were to obey God's laws (including the Ten Commandments) that God had Moses write down.

With David (2 Sam 7) – God will raise up David's offspring and establish his kingdom, which will endure forever before God. In exchange, David was not permitted to build a temple for the Ark of the Covenant or the Lord.

CHRISTIAN LOVE?

As John records (in 1 John 4:8), "God is Love." In a sense, the fundamental message that the apostles were to share with the world is that it's all about *love*. Love of God, love of your neighbor, even love of yourself. But what does it mean to love?

When Jesus was arrested, Peter, while warming himself over a fire and looking across the courtyard at Jesus, denied him three times (John 18). After Jesus was raised, the Lord called Peter over to him, sat him down across from another fire, and gave Peter a chance to redeem himself. Of course, Christ is the true redeemer, but Jesus knew that the feeling of guilt and shame Peter must have felt would be a stumbling block, so Christ provided an opportunity to wash that feeling away and, at the same time, set an example to Peter on how to engage in active compassion. What makes this story particularly interesting is that, in ancient Greek, several different words were used to distinguish different types of love. Before looking at the scripture quoted below, look at some of the different words used by the Greeks and the various types of love they sought to describe. Scholars argue about the significance of the interplay in word usage within this passage, but it is useful to note that there are definitely different types and variations of love.

Ancient Greek Words Translated As *Love*

Agápe – A very deep love, rather than the attractive love suggested by Éros. The kind of love felt for your spouse and children, an unconditional love.

Éros – A passionate love, the type of love triggered by youthful beauty.

Philia – An affectionate love, the type of love in a close friendship, and conveying a sense of loyalty.

Storge – The natural affectionate love felt by parents for their children. Usually used when describing family relationships.

When they had finished eating, Jesus said to Simon Peter, "Simon son of John, do you truly love [agape] me more than these?" "Yes, Lord," he said, "you know that I love [Philia] you." Jesus said, "Feed my lambs." Again Jesus said, "Simon son of John, do you truly love [agape] me?" He answered, "Yes, Lord, you know that I love [Philia] you." Jesus said, "Take care of my sheep." The third time he said to him, "Simon son of John, do you love [Philia] me?" Peter was hurt because Jesus asked him the third time, "Do you love me?" He said, "Lord, you know all things; you know that I love [Philia] you." Jesus said, "Feed my sheep. I tell you the truth, when you were younger you dressed yourself and went where you wanted; but when you are old you will stretch out your hands, and someone else will dress you and lead you where you do not want to go."

– John 21:15-18

A researcher in psychology, Johan Alan Lee, analyzed different types of love in couples and as a result of his research, identified several different love "styles," the definitions of which appear in the box that follows (it looks like he borrowed the names from Greek). This information is included here because, throughout scripture, a recurring analogy of marriage between God and his people (and between Jesus and the church) is presented. We also know from scripture that Jesus loves his church, and we Christians generally say we love Jesus. But what do we mean by that?

Relationship *Love Styles*

Eros – A passionate, romantic love defined by intimacy and a love where partners want to be together spiritually. Eros lovers believe in friendship forever. This type of love can overcome any obstacle.

Ludus – Considers love a playground where it is important to show better qualifications and prove who is more important in the relationship. The focus of the relationship is to satisfy your own needs, and if this cannot be done, the relationship fails.

Storge – Based upon how impressed the participants are with each other. They want to do all things together and spent all time together.

Mania (a combination of Eros and Ludus) – A stressful relationship where partners have a strong need for love and are both obsessed and jealous of each other. Partners have low self-esteem and need constant attention. Relationships, not surprisingly, do not last long.

Pragma (a combination of Ludus and Storge) – A rational, pragmatic love based on practical compatibility.

Agape (a combination of Eros and Storge) – A self-sacrificing love that does not demand reciprocation or respect.

What style of love did the Pharisees have for God? What style of love did Peter have for Jesus? How about Paul? What style of love did they have for each other and for the people who came into their lives? More importantly, of course, is to understand what style of love you have for the Lord and for those around you, both friends and enemies.

If you ask a group of Christians, "Why do you follow Christ?", frequently the answer you will get back is "to make sure I get into heaven." Which of these "love styles" belong to this relationship goal?

A good follow-up question to ask yourself is "if you found out that you weren't going to be allowed into heaven, (like Moses found out he wasn't going to be allowed into the Promised Land –

see Numbers 20:1-13), what would you do differently in life?" Would you still love and serve God anyway? The answer may be indicative of your own love styles for God.

Physiologists have also noted four different phases of love within a marital relationship. The first two are initial attraction and passion, which includes in its definition, that feeling that your partner is completely perfect and can do no wrong.

Developing more slowly, the next phase of love is intimacy, which is forged through time spent together and the maturing of trust through continuing self-revelation and sharing. Also growing more slowly is the fourth phase of love, which is committed love – the love that says *I'll stick by you even though I know you have problems.*

The first two phases of love usually last a few short years; the second two phases of love grow slowly but, if deliberately developed, last a lifetime.

Ask some elders within your small group or at your church if they see any analogies between this type of love within couples, and the type of love they've felt for the Lord through the course of their relationship with Him. How do you go about developing that intimate and committed love for the Lord?

A second recurring analogy to our relationship with God is that of a father and child. Jesus introduced the idea of viewing God as our loving father, or "Daddy" (Mark 14:36). We know that the relationship between a father and child changes as the child matures from early childhood, adolescence, early adulthood, and into full adulthood. Over the course of this time, the role of the father changes from coach, to counselor, to consultant, and finally to colleague and companion.

In some ways, these same phases of the father/son relationship appear to be present in God's relationship with his children corporately, and individually. In Galatians Paul writes:

Therefore the law was our tutor to bring us to Christ, that we might be

justified by faith. But after faith has come, we are no longer under a tutor.
 – Galatians 3:24-25

This passage shows God's relationship with the Israelites in the coaching phase. As you read through Acts, it becomes evident that God intends us to move forward in our maturity and he has provided a Counselor (John 14:26) to aid us in this journey.

Luke's history of this time in the church also appears to document the maturing of Paul's relationship with the Lord as well. In the early years of his ministry, Jesus and the Holy Spirit provide the direction for his ministry, but towards the end, it appears the Holy Spirit has become Paul's consultant, and his view of Jesus becomes one of companionship (Philippians 1:23 – written ~61 AD).

Viewing our relationship with God this way explains the apparent dichotomy between the stern God of the Old Testament and the compassionate God of the New Testament. God has been the same God all along, He has just provided us what we needed at the time.

Any good father provides for his children whatever they need to succeed, to grow, and to mature. However, he will not do for children that which they are able to do for themselves, because that would weaken his children, not strengthen them.

As you read Acts, you will see the Holy Spirit working miracles that help the apostles and early disciples do what they could not do on their own. However, as the apostles and disciples effectively shared the gospel of Jesus through preaching and through the writing of the letters that would eventually become the New Testament, the need for God to do this work diminishes. Some wonder why each new Christian is not endowed with the miraculous powers that Peter, John, and the other apostles were given: It is because our father in heaven loves us, continues to provide for us what we need, and withholds from us that which would weaken or hurt us, just like any loving father would.

THE HOLY SPIRIT

Many theologians discuss the idea that the activities of the Holy Spirit in the world have changed over time. The Holy Spirit is first introduced in the Bible in Genesis 1:2, where we see He is active in the creation process. Throughout the rest of the Bible, the Holy Spirit is shown to have provided supernatural gifts to certain individuals. Examples of these gifts include the providing of knowledge (Neh. 9:20), the enabling of prophecy (Num. 11:16-17), and the enabling of special talents (Ex. 31:2-6). It can be noted that, when these gifts had been given, the purpose had been to serve the general good of the people, rather than provide a specific blessing to an individual. In other words, the gifts were given to enable these individuals to fulfill the Lord's purposes, not their own purposes.

In Acts, we see the Holy Spirit beginning to serve an additional role as the early prophets had predicted (Joel 2:28, Micah 3:8). The Holy Spirit has been poured out onto all people where He works to reveal our sins to us and to make us understand that we are in need of His grace. The Spirit's work of revelation can come in many forms: through the study of the inspired scriptures, through circumstances that cause us to open our hearts in new ways, and through people who the Spirit brings into our lives at the right time, such as occurred with Philip and the Ethiopian (Acts 8:26:39).

Once we acknowledge our sins, repent, and place our faith in Jesus, the Spirit, by the grace of God, *indwells* us, *justifies* us before God, and begins to *sanctify* us. The term *sanctification* refers to the continuing work of the Holy Spirit in our hearts to remove sin from our lives and enable us to grow in our faith.

This indwelling of the Spirit is a new, special gift that was revealed on the day of Pentecost. Indwelling of the Spirit occurred directly from God two notable times in the history of the Church. First, when the Spirit was first given to the Israelites (Acts 2), and second, when the Spirit was first given to the Gentiles (Acts 10). Other than these two special moments in history, the Bible shows us that the indwelling occurs when we are baptized into the Spirit (Acts 2:38-40, Rom 6:3-4, Col 2:12). It is unclear why baptism is necessary, but could it be that God is a god of relationships? Could it be that he doesn't intend for us to walk alone? Baptism into the Spirit is also baptism into the community of believers, the church, the bride of Christ.

The results of this *justification* is that our spirits are regenerated and we are no longer slaves to sin, but through the power of the Holy Spirit within us, we are able to resist sin (Rom 8:1-14).

As we see in Acts, the Holy Spirit's work on our hearts can be resisted before we are indwelled, as King Agrippa demonstrated in Acts 26, and it can also be resisted after we are indwelled, as evidenced by Ananias and Sapphira in Acts 5.

The grace of God is an incredible gift that brings joy, peace and freedom from the pain of sin in our hearts. However, prior to receiving this gift, it is important that you *not* resist the Holy Spirit, but rather invite and allow Him to search your own heart and accept that it contains some ugliness. This may be jealousy, envy, resentment, callousness, greed, or any number of other things that serve to separate you from God. Once you come to terms that this ugliness does exist within you, then it is time to repent and place your faith in Jesus and make the decision to be baptized into a new relationship with the Lord.

In Acts, this new work of God in the world, performed through the Holy Spirit, was heralded with many miracles. Throughout the story of the Bible, we can see that miracles often occurred to demonstrate God's hand in the redemptive works being performed as is evidenced by the lives of Moses, Jesus and, now we see in Acts, the apostles. The story of Moses offers an interesting parallel to that of the apostles. In both cases, the Spirit led these men to commit their testimony of God to the written word and to establish a means for this word to be shared with future generations such as the celebration festivals, and the sharing of the bread and wine in communion.

In the Old Testament, we see that a diminishment of recorded miracles follows the establishment of the Israelites in their promised land. By this time, the hand of God was undeniably demonstrated and the knowledge He had passed to Moses was freely available for His people.

With the formation of the Bible in the 4th century and the establishment of the church through the apostolic preaching throughout the world, do we have a continuing need for miracles in order to understand the message of God? Some theologians (known as *cessationists*) argue that, with the completion of the Bible canon, all miracles stopped; however, isn't the miracle of the Holy Spirit working on our hearts still evident to those who do not resist Him?

Understanding the Holy Spirit and Baptism Through the Marriage Analogy

The marriage analogy that the Bible introduces can be used to help explain better this new relationship with the Lord that begins to reveal itself in Acts.

Earthly marriage has two primary effects: First, at the moment of marriage, we obtain certain legal and social rights. Second, as a healthy marriage continues, our relationship with our spouse causes us to grow and change in new ways.

Considering the first of these effects, as a new spouse, you suddenly have certain social rights not previously held. For example, your spouse may be a member of an exclusive club that you would otherwise not be allowed admittance to; however, invitations to events at these clubs read *for members and their spouses*. Jesus obtained membership rights to His father's house in heaven by living a sinless life. When you become the spiritual "wife" of Jesus, you are also granted the right to enter the father's house.

The legal rights spouses have include property rights. At the moment of marriage, you become co-owners of any assets of your spouse and along with the rights of ownership, you also incur the responsibilities for these assets as well. Upon Jesus' return to heaven after his crucifixion, he inherited the kingdom of God. Therefore, upon our marriage to Jesus, we become co-heirs to the kingdom. As loving spouses, we should also understand that we also inherited the responsibility to grow and nourish this kingdom.

This first effect of marriage is known in theological circles as *justification*, and comes through our relationship with Jesus and was enabled by his sacrifice on the cross for our sins.

The second effect of marriage is the ongoing, transformational aspect of any healthy marriage. Prior to a couple getting married, the focus of life is on taking care of yourself and serving your own needs. Following marriage, this changes; your new focus becomes that of serving the needs of your spouse and your marriage relationship. You begin building intimacy through time spent together and through the continuing, deepening, self-revelations made to each other. When couples get married, they often don't truly understand each other; however, over time, as the intimacy builds through these meaningful conversations and by working together on mutual goals, our knowledge and love for each other grows. Through this process, we seek to encourage one another, build each other up, support one another, and in many (but not all) ways, we give up our prior selves and become like one another.

Within our marriage to the Lord, this is how our relationship with the Holy Spirit works. One way our intimacy with the Lord is expressed is through our prayers and, just as in our human experience, there are times when we simply want to talk in our conversations and other times when we simply want to listen, but all the time we want to know that the other is there with us. The Holy Spirit inspired the written scriptures for our benefit. An especially good way to listen to the Holy Spirit is through the reading and studying of his words. Another way we build our intimacy is through time spent together helping to build the kingdom – serving and sharing the love of our Father with those around us.

This growing together with and through the Holy Spirit is known as *sanctification*.

It is important to understand, however, that just as there are both strong and weak marriages in our earthly realm, so there can be strong and healthy marriages with the Holy Spirit. We can neglect these intimate conversations, we can ignore the words of our spouse, we can continue to act for our own selfish needs. Just as in a human marriage, the joy, peace, and contentment of our spiritual marriage is greatly influenced by the love and care we put into it.

Baptism can be thought of as our Spiritual wedding to the Lord. It is the moment that we confess openly to our friends and families that we want to remain in a committed relationship with this one person, the moment that we renounce our desires for any previous relationships we may have had, and the moment that we obtain the legal rights of a married person.

Some jurisdictions support the idea of common-law marriage. That is, if two people spend enough time together, then the law declares them married and they, therefore, obtain the legal rights of a married person. Among theologians, there is disagreement as to whether or not this same concept applies to our spiritual relationship with Jesus.

However, when choosing whether or not you wish to be baptized, it is worth considering, a little more, the purpose of a wedding ceremony. A wedding ceremony is, in many ways, a loving gift for the parents and family of those getting married. It is a way of letting them know that you care enough about them that you want them in your life and you want them to share this wonderful experience with you.

It is also a distinct and specific time to publicly announce your committed relationship and renounce all past relationships. Most of us know that we are far more likely to keep commitments that we express in public than those that we keep to ourselves. This is because if we choose to go back on our commitment, we won't be held publicly accountable and we won't have to experience the resultant shame or embarrassment.

In a sense, failing to announce your spiritual marriage in public is a way to leave a backdoor open to your relationship with Satan. This is not the type of commitment that is acceptable to the Lord.

TIMELINE OF PAUL'S MISSIONARY LIFE

Year	Event	Reference
5 AD	Paul's birth	
32 AD	Begins persecution of the Church	Acts 7
34 AD	Paul's Conversion	Acts 9
34-36 AD	Paul goes to Arabia and back to Damascus	Gal 1:17
36 AD	Visits apostles in Jerusalem	Gal 1:18
Unknown	Returns to Tarsus	Acts 9:30
43-44 AD	Brought to Antioch by Barnabas	Acts 11:25
45-49 AD	First missionary journey	Acts 13
49-50 AD	Goes back to Jerusalem to discuss theology of Gentiles	Acts 15
50-52 AD	Second missionary journey	Acts 15-18
51-52 AD	Writes 1 Thessalonians and 2 Thessalonians	
53-58 AD	Third missionary journey	Acts 18
53 AD	Visits Phyrgia and Galatia	Acts 18:23
54-57 AD	Visits Ephesus	Acts 19
55 AD	Writes Galatians	
56 AD	Writes 1 Corinthians	
57 AD	Visits Macedonia	Acts 20:1-2
57 AD	Writes 2 Corinthians	
57-58 AD	Visits Corinth	Acts 20:2-3
58 AD	Writes Romans	

Year	Event	Reference
58 AD	Goes back to Jerusalem with offerings for the poor and is arrested	Acts 21,22,23
58-60 AD	Imprisoned by Felix in Caesarea	Acts 24,25
58	Preaches to Felix	Acts 24
60 AD	Preaches to Festus and Agrippa II	Acts 25
60-61 AD	Paul sent to Rome	Acts 27,28
61-63 AD	Paul preaches while under house arrest	Acts 28
61 AD	Writes Ephesians, Philippians, Colossians, and Philemon	
63 AD	Paul released from Prison	
63-67	Paul continues missionary work, possibly going to Spain	Romans 15:24,28
63 AD	Writes 1 Timothy	
65	Writes Titus	
67	Paul Arrested again	
67	Paul writes 2 Timothy from prison	
~67	Paul beheaded under Nero	
70	Romans destroy the temple, signaling the end of the Jewish age	

Note that the dates shown in the table above are approximate, and scholarly debate continues on the exact dates of the various events in the apostle's life.

ACTS 1 - 4

Acts opens with an account of the last encounter the disciples had with the resurrected Jesus in the flesh. Following this, we have the introduction of the Holy Spirit, which serves as the starting point for the true Christian church, and a description of Peter's early leadership of the church in Jerusalem.

1) In Acts 1:6, what question did the disciples ask Jesus? What does this say about their understanding of His ministry? What were they expecting? What kingdom was Jesus here to restore?

2) Jesus was crucified on the day of the Feast of Unleavened Bread (when an unblemished lamb was sacrificed for the forgiveness of sins), His resurrection occurred on the Feast of First Fruits (see also 1 Cor 15:20-23). In Jewish tradition, the Feast of Pentecost (also known as the Feast of Weeks) commemorates God giving the Ten Commandments on Mount Sinai. This is the very day

that Jesus sent forth his Holy Spirit. Why all these coincidences? What does it mean?

3) Acts 1:14 indicates that *they were all joined together constantly in prayer.* (Refer also to Acts 4:32, Psalms 133.) Does this imply that the Lord desires unity of spirit amongst his followers? Is this a pattern we should replicate? Throughout Acts, does it show other instances where the apostles worked to build unity?

4) In Acts 1:15-26 we see Peter had decided to appoint another apostle to fulfill a prophecy in Scripture. Was it Peter's job to do this? Did Jesus himself also appoint another apostle (Galatians 1:1)? Compare Peter's actions with Sarah's (Gen 15:4,16:2). Did God end up blessing both Ishmael and Isaac?

5) Did some in the crowd offer a worldly explanation for the miraculous events following the coming of the Holy Spirit (Acts 2:13)? Does this trend continue today?

6) In Acts 2:38, Peter tells the people to repent. The Greek word used is *metanoeo*, which means *to change one's mind, i.e. to repent to change one's mind for better, heartily to amend with abhorrence of one's past sins* (see also Rom 12:2). Is this what you thought repent meant? How do you go about "changing your mind"? About what? What does this mean to you in your own life?

7) How many believers did Jesus gather (John 6:60-71, Acts 1:15)? How many believers did Peter gather from his first sermon (Acts 2:41)? What does this say about our different ministerial roles (see Luke 10:2)? What does this say about Jesus' relationship with God and our relationship with God (see Rom 8:17)?

8) In Acts 3, how frequently was the crippled man laid at the temple? How often was Jesus himself at the temple (Mark 14:49)? What do these two facts imply? What does this tell you about miracles?

9) In Acts 4, the priests and Sadducees grabbed John and Peter when they talked about the resurrection of Jesus. What memories did this sermon recall for them (Mathew 22:23-33)? Do you think that the priests, the temple guard, and the Sadducees would have not noticed the miracle Peter and John just performed in the temple? What mental processes would drive them to disbelieve such important truths? Are any of these same mental processes at work in your own mind?

10) How could simple fishermen like Peter and John share God's word so effectively (Acts 4:8) and with such courage? What was it about Peter and John that enabled the Holy Spirit to come to them and work through them? What lessons can we learn from them?

11) We all have priorities in life; usually our priorities are most evidenced by how we spend our time and money. What were the priorities of these first Christians (Acts 4:32-37)? What were they expecting (Acts 1:6, Mathew 25:1-13)? Are Christians really called to sell all they own and give it away? What should guide us in these decisions? What are your priorities?

ACTS 5-8

Acts 5 opens with an account of the first believers who turned away from the Lord and moves on with an account of the continued growth and administration of the early church. Next, we learn of Stephen, the first martyr of the church, and close with an introduction to Saul, the persecutor.

1) In Isaiah 54:5 we read: *For your Maker is your husband – the LORD Almighty is his name – the Holy One of Israel is your Redeemer; he is called the God of all the earth.* This is part of a recurring analogy of God as husband of his people. In Ephesians 5:22-33, (particularly verse 32), we see this analogy continued between Jesus and the church. Within a relationship, what does God consider unforgivable (see Mathew 5:31)? In Acts 5:3, we can assume from the context, that Ananias and Sapphira were believers, recently baptized with the Holy Spirit. What Spirit did Ananias let into his heart? Using this marriage analogy, how did God view Ananias's and Sapphira's actions? What happened do them?

2) In Acts 5, we see the Sanhedrin rejects the message of Peter and the Apostles as they had rejected the message of Jesus. How is it that people so focused on seeking and following God can

completely miss Him? Can this still happen today?

3) What was the name of the one Pharisee who expressed reason in the Sanhedrin? (Note: The Sanhedrin was essentially the Jewish supreme court.) What was his argument? How would history reflect on this argument?

Note: We will hear more from a student of this Pharisee later in the narrative.

4) In Acts 5:41, what did the apostles rejoice over? Why did they rejoice over this? (To help understand this, think of a second string athlete whose coach suddenly chooses them to play in the big game.) Did Peter and the other apostles deliberately set out to suffer pain, or was their suffering simply an unavoidable consequence of preaching the Gospel? Does the Bible anywhere tell Christians to deliberately try to hurt themselves or get themselves hurt?

5) In Acts 6, we see the first recorded division of duties within the Christian church, which was prompted by an awareness of ethnic discrimination in the distribution of food. Does the text say that this dividing of duties was prompted by the Holy Spirit or by man? Was it in any way wrong for the apostles to organize the disciples this way? What three duties are mentioned? What

effect did this have on the ministry (Acts 6:7)?

6) What Job was Stephen given during this organization of works? What was he accused of (Acts 6:13)? Although the testimony of his accusers was misleading, it probably held many seeds of truth. Do you think Stephen was silent and businesslike in his assigned duties? If not, what else do you think he was doing? Are you the same way as you live your life?

7) In Chapter 7, Stephen was able to give a powerful summary of his faith. Why do you think Luke recorded this whole speech? Do you think he accurately summarized the good news (gospel) of Jesus? Are you prepared to do the same (see 1 Pet 3:15)?

8) Was the Holy Spirit active before Pentecost (Acts 7:51)?

9) What was Stephen's response to his executioners (Acts 7:61)? What was the relationship between Stephen and Jesus (See Luke 23:34 and then John 17:23)? What would you like your relationship to Jesus be like? Do you have this same automatic response to those who hurt you?

10) What was Saul's role in Stephen's death (Acts 8)? Stephen was, as they say, the straw that broke the camel's back for the Pharisees. What did Stephen motivate Saul to do? What were Saul's underlying motivations for his actions? Have you ever done evil because you were thinking self-righteously?

11) In Acts 8:3, we see that the early church was meeting in the homes of individuals. We will see this pattern throughout the rest of Acts and the New Testament. What different dynamics exist in a home church verses a church that meets in a building? Are there differences in the type of work involved in those doing ministry (e.g., think of the logistical effort it takes to maintain a church building)? Did the early churches have a need for separate small group meetings? Do we have a need today?

12) What was the effect of the persecution (Acts 8:4)? Who was in Jerusalem at the time (Acts 2:5)? What were they doing prior to this (Acts 2:44)? What did Jesus predict (Mathew 24:14) would happen with His Gospel? Recall the story of Joseph and read Genesis 37:14-17. Does God ever influence events to fulfill his purposes?

13) Who preached the good news of Jesus? Was it just the designated apostles (Acts 8:4)? Whom does the Holy Spirit guide in thought and word (Act 7)? Who is supposed to be sharing the good news and helping people see the wonderful light of God (see 1 Peter 2:9)? Who is supposed to be interpreting the scriptures for you?

14) What is the price that God demands that we pay for a redeemed relationship with him (Acts 8:18-23)?

15) When should a person be baptized (Acts 8:37)? What does baptism do (Acts 2:38)?

ACTS 9-12

In this lesson, we learn of Paul's conversion and his calling to be an apostle to the Gentiles and an account of his first preaching. We also see Peter getting his first understanding that the new covenant with Jesus supersedes, or fulfills, the earlier covenants God made with Abraham, Moses, and David.

1) What was Saul's response to Jesus?

2) Did Ananias have cause to be worried about what the Lord was telling him to do (Acts 9:13-14)? What was Ananias's response (Acts 9:17)? Have you ever been afraid to do something the Lord was prompting you to do? Did you ever chicken out and simply not follow the prompting? What consequences did you fear? Were they comparable to what Ananias feared? What happened to you after you ignored the Lord's request, and how did you feel in spirit?

3) What do you think was going through Saul's mind for the three days after he was blinded (Acts 9:9)? Was he angry at his blindness, bitter, what?

4) What did Paul do immediately after he got his sight back?

5) God continually challenges us to grow, to change, and to renew our minds; humans, however, cherish consistency and stability – we resist the efforts to change our worldview. What was Saul's response to this new view of Jesus? What is your response when you learn a little more about Jesus?

6) In Acts 9:23-25, we find that Saul had to run for his life after his short preaching stint. Where did he go after leaving (read Saul's personal testimony in Galatians 1:11-24)? Scholars believe he

stayed in Arabia for three years before returning to Damascus, but neither Acts nor Paul's own letters record any activities he might have been doing in this time. What do you think someone like Paul might have been doing in this time (See Acts 5:34,18:28, 22:3)?

7) Saul persecuted the followers in Jerusalem, personally arresting and imprisoning friends and family members of the disciples (Acts 8:3), and he even helped kill their close friend Stephen. What was their response to him when they saw him next (Acts 9:26-29)? How would you feel about inviting someone who did this to your friends and family into your home to stay and bond with you? What limitations are there to your love? What limitations are there to the love Jesus has for you?

8) In verses 9:29-30, we learn of Saul debating with the Grecian Jews, which caused strife and therefore caused the brothers to send him out of the region. In verse 31, we hear that the region then enjoyed a time of peace. Was verse 31 intended as humor in any way? Can we learn anything from this about balancing the need to be right with the need to build strong relationships?

NOTE: During this period in history, Jewish communities existed in towns and areas throughout the Roman Empire. Within these communities, they built synagogues that served as much as a community center as a place for worship. Gentiles were welcomed into these centers and over time came to learn and appreciate many aspects of the Jewish faith. One of the reasons the apostles were able to be so successful in spreading the message was that many Gentiles where already prepared, to some extent, to hear the message of God and were thankful to the invitation that Jesus gave them to restore and participate in a relationship with the Lord. Acts 10 introduces us to such a man.

9) Was Cornelius a Jew (Acts 10:28)? Was God willing or desirous to have a relationship with Cornelius, even though he did not follow the covenant agreements God made with Abraham (circumcision), or Moses (the Mosaic Law)? How did Cornelius live his life? What motivated him to live this way? Prior to the events recorded in Chapter 10, what promises from God, would Cornelius be counting on as reward for his lifestyle? Are you only interested in following a Christian lifestyle because of rewards you might get?

10) The Mosaic Law included strict guidelines about what to eat and what not to eat. The dietary restrictions recorded in Acts 10:12 includes animals that were specifically defined in Leviticus 11 as being unclean and were to never be eaten by an Israelite. What message was God trying to convey to Peter about the Mosaic Law? Was the timing of this particular vision a coincidence?

11) In Acts 10:16, we learn that God gave the same vision to Peter three times in a row. Why was this (see Mathew 16:22, 17:4, 26:33, John 1:42, 21:15-18)? (Note that *Peter*, or *Petros*, means *rock* or *stone*.)

12) What did Peter realize in Acts (10:34-35, 43)?

13) In this narrative, who was astonished (10:45), and what did they find so particularly astonishing?

14) In Acts 11:1-3, with whom did Peter have discord and why? What was their response (Acts 11:18)? Have you ever known a group of people, wholly committed to a particular viewpoint in life, to change their mind on it after a single conversation?

15) Luke records in detail the story of Peter and Cornelius, and then he records in detail the story of Peter telling the story. Luke also takes care to document the fact that there were multiple witnesses to these events. Why did Luke go to all this trouble?

16) Was God OK with his message being preached to the Gentiles (Acts 11:21)?

17) What is baptism with water all about (1 Peter 3:18-22)? Was it important to Jesus (Mark 1:1-13)? Was it considered important by the early disciples (Acts 2:38, 8:36, 10:47)?

18) In Acts 9:29-9:30, we learned how those in Jerusalem rejected Paul. Every evangelist understands that the gospel of Jesus will be rejected by many but, in this case, the church didn't reject

Jesus; they rejected Paul himself. How do you think this made Paul feel? Paul must have heard how well the church thrived after he was forced away, how would this kind of news affect his personal motivation and sense of value and purpose? In Acts 11:22-26, we learn that, even though Barnabas was preaching successfully in Antioch, he decided to get Saul. How far do you think he had to walk to check on his old colleague? Do you think Barnabas found a way to apply Jesus' example of redemption? Do you think Barnabas's outreach at this moment of time affected the story of Paul's life? Do you find ways of reaching out to your brothers and sisters who may have become disconnected from your fellowship?

19) What calamity did Agabus predict (Acts 11:28)?

20) In Acts 12:6, we learn that an angel of the Lord helped Peter to escape prison. What activity preceded this miraculous intervention?

21) Why did the chronicler of this escape mention that Rhoda didn't open the door for Peter, even though she recognized who he was?

22) Did the church have great faith that God would respond to their prayers (Acts 12:15)?

23) What happens to a Roman guard who lets a prisoner escape (Acts 12:19)? The Bible includes many other examples (Acts 15:4, Dan 3:22). Are you surprised that God's plans often include "collateral damage" (See Rom 9:21, Job 40)?

24) As God works in your life, what should your response be (Luke 17:15-18)? How does God feel about us accepting praise that should be directed at him (Acts 12:21-22)? If you ever find yourself in this situation, what would a more appropriate response be (Acts 14:11-18)?

ACTS 13-16

Acts 13 begins with Paul and Barnabas embarking on their first missionary journey. We next become witnesses of the first theological debates of the early Christian church as it struggles to understand itself and the attempts made by all parties to maintain unity. Finally, we learn of the rocky start to Paul's second missionary journey.

1) What communal activity did the church do for Paul and Barnabas prior to them leaving for a missionary journey?

2) What did Paul and Barnabas use as their guide on their missionary journey (13:4)?

3) Commentaries often note that Paul preached to the lower classes within society. Within the text, what types of people do we find Paul preaching to in his journeys (Acts 13:7, 16:13, 16:14, 16:34, 18:7, Romans 16:23)?

4) What is God's view of sorcery (Acts 13:10-11, 19:19, 2 Chronicles 33:6, Malachi 3:5)?

5) John Mark, author of the Gospel of Mark, joined Paul on his first missionary trip. Who was he (Acts 12:12, Col 4:10)? What was John's role (Acts 13:5)? How did John fair on the journey (Acts 13:13)?

6) How was Paul and Barnabas's message received (Acts 13:43, 45, 48)? How is it received today?

Note: There has been an ongoing debate in the church about *free will* as opposed to *pre-destination*. Acts 13:48, on the surface, seems to indicate that God has appointed only certain individuals for eternal life. For a counter-verse, read Jesus' words in Mathew 11:28. If you get really stuck on it, refer again to Job 40.

7) What was Paul's and Barnabas's response to the rejection of God's invitation (Acts 13:51-52, Luke 9:5)? The Koran teaches that people should be forced, even to the point of death, to follow God. During the Catholic Church's inquisition in the 12th century, people were tortured until they confessed faith in Jesus. The thinking was that the gift of eternal life was so important that the torturers were really doing their victims a favor. Is this Jesus' guidance for evangelism? (Luke 9:52-56)?

8) Stoning was the traditional means of execution for the Jewish people: They knew how to do it. In Acts 14:19, we learn that

Paul and Barnabas were stoned until the Jews believed them dead. Do you think it hurt? What shape do you think their bodies were in after that? How long do you think it hurt? What other types of suffering did Paul encounter in his preaching (2 Cor 11:25)? What caused Paul and Barnabas to continue preaching (Acts 19:11)? For what purpose does God demonstrate himself through miracles? Do you pray for miracles in your own life? Do you understand the implications of this (Luke 12:48)? Are you ready?

9) Paul and Barnabas worked hard to win converts but, after winning converts, what was happening (Acts 14:19)? What did Paul and Barnabas do to try to prevent people from going astray (Acts 14:23)? Did God tell them to do this? Did God prevent it?

10) Compare the personalities of Paul and Barnabas. Do you believe that their missionary journey would have been as effective if they were not working together?

11) At the end of their first journey, they arrived at Antioch and shared with the disciples how God opened the door to the Gentiles. Acts 15 describes a heated argument between Paul and Barnabas and the followers from Judea. What was the root cause of the argument?

12) Was Peter, himself, faithful to his original vision of openness to the Gentiles (Galatians 2:11-21)? What kind of leadership was Peter providing? What would cause him to "slip"? What would

cause you to "slip"?

13) In Acts 15:19, it appears as if an agreement was reached between Paul and the followers in Jerusalem. Whose judgment was announced? Was it God's? Does the decision articulated in Acts 15:19-21 have the same tone as words spoken by Jesus or the Angel of the Lord, or does it sound more like a political agreement between men? Compare the judgment of James to the advice Paul wrote in 1 Cor 8 (particularly 1 Cor 8:9.) Do you think Paul learned anything from James?

14) What was Paul's view of the encounter (read Galatians 2:1-10)? Recall the famine predicted by Agabus in Acts 11:28. Paul's account includes a part of the agreement not mentioned in Acts – providing gifts for the poor. Do you think money is ever used as leverage in church politics today? Do you think that followers ever struggle to listen to the voice of the Spirit while at the same time, use those skills and talents that have been given to them? Do you think your own life in ministry, whatever your calling, will be any different?

15) Does it sound like the Jerusalem contingent trusted Paul and Barnabas to bring the words of the agreement back to Antioch (Acts 15:22)?

16) Does it sound like Christian theology was well defined and understood at this time in history? Is it possible for news of the grace offered by God to be shared and to bless the lives of people, even with internal personal and theological conflicts

within the church?

17) What was Paul's view of commitment (Acts 15:36-39)? Do you think he had a sense of passion about his ministry? Note: In Colossians 4:10, we have evidence that Paul's relationship with Barnabas and Mark was restored.

18) In these days, it was common for men to go to the local gymnasiums where they did athletic training, socializing and engaging in intellectual discussions. The standard of the day, though, was to undress completely when going into the gym. This meant that, for the Gentiles, circumcision was a publicly displayed commitment: They could not hide it. Why, after all Paul's arguments, did he circumcise Timothy (See 1 Corinthians 9:19-23)?

19) How do you think the Holy Spirit kept Paul from preaching in Asia (Acts 16:6)? How do you know when it is Satan keeping you from doing good, or the Holy Spirit protecting you from harm?

20) How did Paul and Silas handle captivity? How did they use their time behind bars (Acts 16:25)? What do you think they were praying for? Their own needs?

21) Why did the jailor want to kill himself (16:27)?

22) What was Paul's view towards the people around him? Does it sound like he and Silas were always looking for an opportunity to bless those around them?

23) The jailor's conversion experience seems similar to Paul's, although there is no recorded history of the life of this jailor. What effects to you think this experience might have had on the people within his circle of influence?

24) Within the Roman Empire, those who were citizens had significant rights, including the right to a trial, while non-citizens had no such rights. What does Acts 16:37 tell us about Paul's personality?   Who seemed to be the dominate force in the Paul/Silas duo (Acts 17:14)?

25) Could the jailor have been subjected to criticism for hosting prisoners in his home? Would the judges be more, or less, willing to criticize the jailer after being forced to publicly admit their illegal treatment of Paul?

ACTS 17-22

Acts 17 continues the account of Paul's second missionary journey. This lesson then continues with the account of his third missionary journey and concludes with his arrest in Jerusalem.

1) What response did the Bereans have to this new message of Paul's (Acts 17:11)?

2) In Acts, we learn that Paul preached from the Hebrew Scriptures when teaching about God. When confronted with the Greeks, who lived by philosophy and reason, how did Paul preach to them (17:18-33)? What can we learn from Paul about this? Did Jesus take this same approach?

| Luke 6:3-5 – Jesus speaks to Pharisees like a lawyer. |
| Luke 6:17-49 – Jesus speaks to plain folks with plain talk. |
| Luke 7:18-23 – Jesus speaks to disciples about discipleship. |
| Luke 10:41 – Jesus speaks to a woman about feelings. |

3) How did Paul finance his missionary journeys (Acts 18:3, 20:34)?

4) Paul, out of frustration, made a firm and public decision about the future of his ministry (Acts 18:6), but the Lord let Paul know He had different ideas (Acts 18:9) and, to Paul's credit, he listened. What lessons can we draw from Paul's experience?

Note: Acts 19:9 is the first time in scripture that the Christian movement is called "the way".

5) In Mark 16:17, Jesus prophesies that believers will drive out demons "in my name". This does not mean that we can just add the words "in Jesus' name" to anything we say. Jesus is referring to believers who, through baptism, were indwelled with the Holy Spirit. Doing something "in the name of Jesus" implies that the activity we are doing was prompted by the Holy Spirit and in reality, any miraculous outcomes are a result of God's power manifested through His Spirit. What happened when the seven sons of Sceva invoked Jesus' name (Acts 19:15-16)? Why did this happen?

6) These events caused the faith of many followers to deepen. What was their response to their deepened faith (Acts 19:18-19)?

7) Why did Paul send Timothy and Erastus to Macedonia (Rom 16:23, Acts 19:22)?

8) People are fervent about their faith in God. If your preaching meddles with their beliefs, they get upset, but many find they can ignore you. What is it that people just won't ignore if you threaten it (Acts 19:25)?

9) In the great mayhem described in Acts 19:32, why were most people there? Does it remind you of the civil riots in our own time?

10) Was Paul's style of preaching different from that of many pastors today (Acts 20:7-9)?

11) What was Paul's big fear as he saw his ministry coming to a close (Acts 20:29-31)? Are the problems he feared then, still problems now?

12) In Acts 20:27-38, we find that Paul's companions wept for him at their parting. We see this sort of affection shown for Paul elsewhere in the scriptures as well. If your local pastor retired or moved to another church, would you find yourself weeping? How did Paul build such affectionate relationships with people? Is this a pattern we should follow?

13) Through Acts, we see Paul modeling for us both toughness and intimacy. Do you have trouble following Paul's example with either of these aspects? What steps are you taking to develop

these relationship skills?

14) What did Paul encourage these men to do (Acts 20:28)? Do we still have this responsibility today? Do you see yourself as a sheep or as a shepherd?

15) Do you think the Holy Spirit was trying to dissuade Paul from going to Jerusalem, or simply preparing him (Acts 20:22-24, 21:4, 21:10)? Recall that Paul had made a personal commitment to the brothers in Jerusalem to bring back an offering (Galatians 2:1-10). Was it Paul's own pride or stubbornness that caused him to continue on with the offering himself, or the Spirit? In Acts 16:6 we see the Holy Spirit *preventing* Paul from continuing on with his plans, in contrast to this period where the Holy Spirit simply *warns* Paul of the consequences. Could this simply reflect a maturing relationship between Paul and the Spirit?

Note: It was the same prophet Agabus who predicted Paul's arrest in Acts 21:11 that accurately predicted the famine in Act 11:28.

16) Recall the early confrontation between Paul and the followers within Jerusalem. Does it sound like the earlier arguments were resolved (Acts 21:20-22)?

17) How well was Paul's testimony received by the crowd in Jerusalem? Do you think he knew how well it would be received? Do you think he cared how well it would be received? Why?

76

18) It appears that James and the elders have a more mature view of the faith than the flock that they shepherd (Acts 21:18-25). Do you think this makes their role as church leaders more difficult? In what ways? Within your own local church, have most people read the whole Bible?

19) Why was the Roman commander alarmed that he had put a Roman citizen in chains and almost flogged him (Acts 22:23-29)?

Note: In Acts 21:39, the commander thought Paul was the Egyptian who started a revolt. The Jewish historian Josephus, in his *Wars of the Jews*, records that during the time of Felix's rule, an Egyptian, pretending to be a false prophet, deluded thirty thousand men to follow him up to the Mount of Olives in an attempt to overpower the Romans. The false prophet escaped when the Romans came out and successfully quelled the revolt.

Jesus warned the disciples that false prophets would appear during this time (Mathew 24:11).

ACTS 23-28

Following Paul's arrest, we learn how he preached in the courts of kings and built relationships with all that he came in contact with on his way to prison in Rome.

1) Do you think Paul knew how to manipulate the passions of people (Acts 23:6)?

2) In Acts 23:11, the Lord speaks to Paul and gives him encouragement. See also Mathew 10:16-18. Do you think the Lord's hands guided these events?

3) In 24:5, the high priest with the elders accused Paul of stirring up trouble all over the world. The Greek word used here for world was *oikoumene*, the same word used in Mathew 24:14. Does it appear that Jesus' prophecies were beginning to be realized?

4) The historian Josephus, in his work *Antiquities of the Jews*, tells us that Felix lived in adultery with Drusilla who was married to someone else. In Acts 24:22, we learn that Felix was "well acquainted with *The Way*", and in Acts 24:24, we learn that he brought his wife in and wanted to hear more about Jesus Christ. Why do you think Felix became afraid as Paul was speaking to him through the Holy Spirit (Acts 24:25, John 16:8)? Have you ever felt yourself pushing God away because you didn't want to let go of something that was coming between you and Him?

5) What was Felix's response to the position he found himself in? Was his response a wise response? Have you ever felt yourself at the same crossroads?

6) There is saying within the bureaucratic levels of government that you should "never waste a good crisis". Each time Paul appeared before the various kings of the region, Felix, Festus, and Agrippa II, he could have easily been sentenced to death. However, did he waste this crisis by simply giving a defense of his charges (Acts 24:24-25, 26:4-23) ?

Note: Josephus indicated that King Agrippa was a wise and admirable man. His writings also indicated that his wife Bernice was a devout Jew.

7) What do you think of King Agrippa's response to Paul in 26:28? Do you think Paul had any affect (1 Corinthians 3:6)?

8) In Act 27:3, the Roman centurion "allowed him to go to his friends". Do you think that this was normal for a centurion to do with his prisoners? What would have happened to the centurion if Paul escaped? Why do you think the centurion did this (see also Acts 27:31, 27:42-43)?

9) In Acts 28:3-6, we learn that a poisonous snake bit Paul. Why did he not die (Mark 16:18)? Does either of these verses indicate, in any way at all, that a Christian should deliberately go near a poisonous snake?

10) In Acts 28:7-9, how many islanders were miraculously cured? Do you think this escaped the notice of the Roman guards? Note that in 380 AD, the *Edict of Thessalonica* declared Christianity the Roman Empire's sole authorized religion. Do you think Paul was concerned about long time frames?

11) While on his missionary tours, Paul always went to the synagogues first to start preaching the good news. Under house arrest in Rome, what did Paul do first (Acts 28:17,23)? What did he do after that (Acts 28:30)?

12) Paul spent many years of his life in custody. On a day-to-day basis, how did you think he spent his time? What was his focus? Do you think he saw this time as an opportunity?

13) How much of his emotional energy did Paul put into his mission? How much of his physical energy? How much of his intellectual energy? Do you think he invested all his money in a safe mutual fund portfolio? What are you willing to give over to God to spread his Grace to others?

14) As you look across the history of the Jewish people from Noah to Jesus, you can discern God unfolding a grand plan. Who did God do all this for? In the gospels, we learn how Jesus came to Earth and poured out his life. Who did he do this for? In Acts, we read how Paul crisscrossed the world, walking hundreds of miles, possibly spending up to 25% of his life in prison and enduring countless other hardships. Who did he do this for? Have you ever lost someone close to you and wished you could have them back? Do you understand?

The introductory material of this study guide contains a number of questions about the type of love the apostles demonstrated for the Lord, each other, and others they met, both friends and enemies. To close out this study, take time to review and discuss these questions based on your more in depth understanding of the Acts.

How did the Holy Spirit shape and transform the hearts of the early apostles and disciples to enable a greater love?

Made in the USA
San Bernardino, CA
29 June 2015